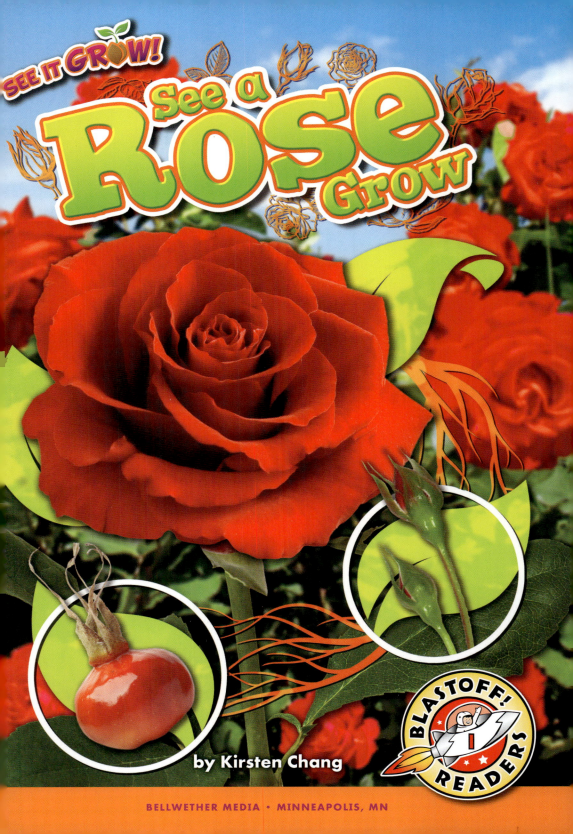

SEE IT GROW!
See a Rose Grow

by Kirsten Chang

BLASTOFF! READERS

BELLWETHER MEDIA • MINNEAPOLIS, MN

Blastoff! Readers are carefully developed by literacy experts to build reading stamina and move students toward fluency by combining standards-based content with developmentally appropriate text.

 Level 1 provides the most support through repetition of high-frequency words, light text, predictable sentence patterns, and strong visual support.

 Level 2 offers early readers a bit more challenge through varied sentences, increased text load, and text-supportive special features.

 Level 3 advances early-fluent readers toward fluency through increased text load, less reliance on photos, advancing concepts, longer sentences, and more complex special features.

★ **Blastoff! Universe**

Reading Level

 Grade K 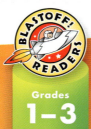 Grades 1–3  Grade 4

This edition first published in 2024 by Bellwether Media, Inc.

No part of this publication may be reproduced in whole or in part without written permission of the publisher. For information regarding permission, write to Bellwether Media, Inc., Attention: Permissions Department, 6012 Blue Circle Drive, Minnetonka, MN 55343.

Library of Congress Cataloging-in-Publication Data

LC record for See a Rose Grow available at: https://lccn.loc.gov/2023000696

Text copyright © 2024 by Bellwether Media, Inc. BLASTOFF! READERS and associated logos are trademarks and/or registered trademarks of Bellwether Media, Inc.

Editor: Elizabeth Neuenfeldt   Designer: Brittany McIntosh

Printed in the United States of America, North Mankato, MN.

Table of Contents

Sweet Flowers	4
How Do They Grow?	6
Fully Grown	18
Glossary	22
To Learn More	23
Index	24

Sweet Flowers

Roses are colorful flowers. They grow on bushes. They smell sweet!

How Do They Grow?

A rose grows from a small seed. The seed is planted in soil.

seeds

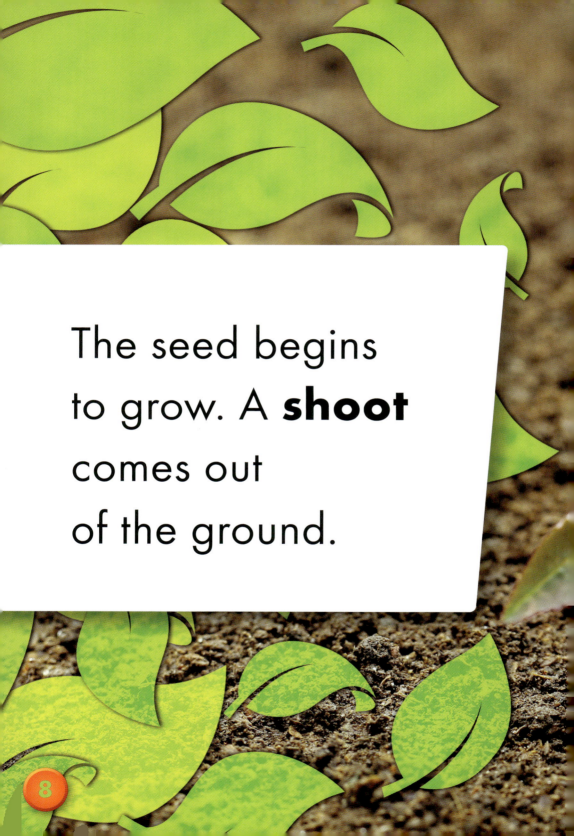

The seed begins to grow. A **shoot** comes out of the ground.

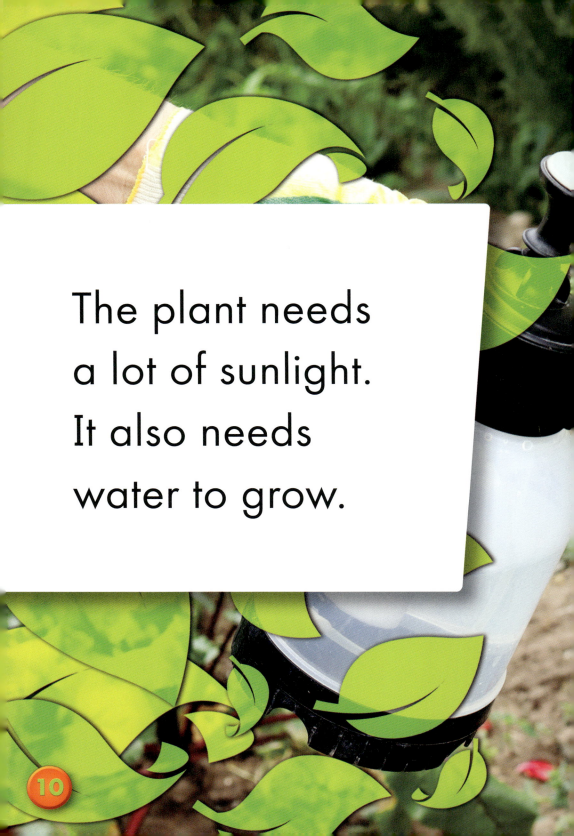

The plant needs a lot of sunlight. It also needs water to grow.

The plant gets bigger. Leaves and **buds** form.

The buds **bloom** into roses.
Bees **pollinate** the flowers.

bee pollinating a rose

Rose hips begin to form. They hold seeds!

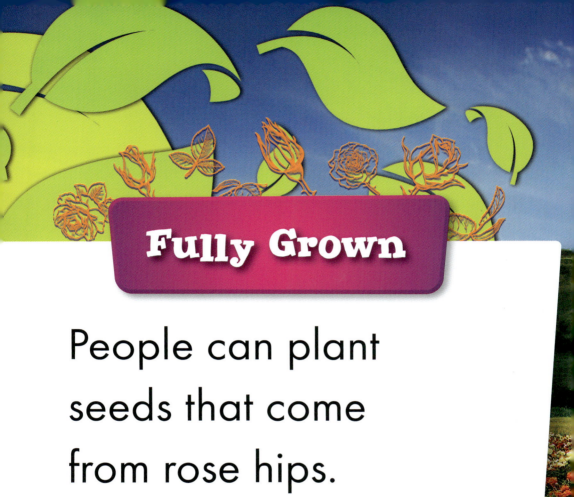

Fully Grown

People can plant seeds that come from rose hips. More roses will grow!

Roses can be used in **bouquets**. They look very pretty!

Glossary

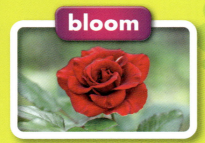
bloom — to open into a flower

pollinate — to move a dust called pollen to make seeds grow

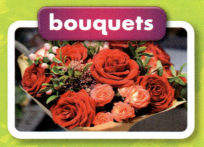
bouquets — groupings of cut flowers

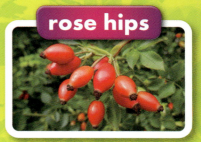
rose hips — pods where rose seeds grow

buds — growths that turn into flowers

shoot — part of a new plant that grows above the ground

To Learn More

AT THE LIBRARY

Chang, Kirsten. *See a Sunflower Grow.* Minneapolis, Minn.: Bellwether Media, 2023.

Peters, Katie. *Spring Flowers.* Minneapolis, Minn.: Lerner Publications, 2020.

Press, J.P. *Spring Plants.* Minneapolis, Minn.: Bearport Publishing, 2022.

ON THE WEB

FACTSURFER

Factsurfer.com gives you a safe, fun way to find more information.

1. Go to www.factsurfer.com.
2. Enter "see a rose grow" into the search box and click 🔍.
3. Select your book cover to see a list of related content.

Index

bees, 14, 15
bloom, 14
bouquets, 20, 21
buds, 12, 13, 14
bushes, 4
flowers, 4, 14
ground, 8
leaves, 12
life cycle, 19
needed to grow, 11
plant, 10, 12, 18
pollinate, 14, 15
rose hips, 16, 17, 18

seed, 6, 7, 8, 16, 17, 18
shoot, 8, 9
smell, 4
soil, 6
sunlight, 10
using roses, 21
water, 10

The images in this book are reproduced through the courtesy of: Tiger Images, front cover (rose), p. 3; Lukas Gojda, front cover (rose bud); Picture Partners, front cover (rose hip); Anita Ben, pp. 4-5; Pete Pahham, pp. 6-7; Heike Rau, p. 7 (inset); Mohammed Anwarul Kabir Choudhury/ Alamy, pp. 8-9; Tasha-photo, pp. 10-11; Nik Merkulov, p. 11 (soil); rangizzz, p. 11 (sunlight); Mariia Boiko, p. 11 (water); Andrew Swarga, pp. 12-13; KOOKOO, pp. 14-15; awol666, p. 15 (inset); Sophie McAulay, pp. 16-17; Sandra Ciccarelli, p. 17 (inset); stock09, pp. 18-19; martapskov, pp. 20-21; Africa Studio, p. 21 (oils, perfumes); Luchi_a, p. 21 (bouquets); lola_art, p. 22 (bloom); Aleksandr_Alekseev, p. 22 (bouquets); Michael Osmolovsky, p. 22 (buds); Joe Kirby Photography, p. 22 (pollinate); Fabian Junge, p. 22 (rose hips); Kanokorn 5914, p. 22 (shoot); Egor Rodynchenko, p. 23.